Dockmanship

Dockmanship

BY

DAVID OWEN BELL

MASTER MARINER

Cornell Maritime Press

Centreville, Maryland

Illustrations are by the author.

Library of Congress Cataloging-in-Publication Data

Bell, David Owen.
    Dockmanship / David Owen Bell.—1st ed.
        p. cm.
    Includes index.
    ISBN 0-87033-425-5 (pbk.)
    1. Boats and boating. 2. Mooring of ships. I. Title.
VK545.B45 1991
623.8'62—dc20   91-55483
                                                            CIP

Manufactured in the United States of America

First edition, 1992; second printing, 1994

To my daughter and my parents,
and to the memory of Nicholas S. Benton,
Master Rigger

Contents

Introduction

Dock·man·ship\\' dok-mən-₁ ship \ *n*: the art, skill, and practice of safely berthing and unberthing a vessel

Docking modern pleasure boats should be easy. They generally have plenty of power for their size, responsive steering, and unobstructed views. Why, then, do some people find it so difficult?

Most people dock by trial and error. There's no one to teach them, and after a clumsy landing in front of an audience, they're too embarrassed to ask for help or to analyze what went wrong. With an understanding of how boats behave in close quarters, most skippers can learn to plan and execute the maneuver with skill.

The components of any docking situation fall into one of three categories. First are the elements under your control that can be expected to respond predictably: the engine, the rudder, and the dock lines. Next are the external forces beyond your control: wind and current. In some areas, these elements may form a prevailing pattern, but their essence is generally one of change. Finally, there is the human factor. This is an area partially under your control and includes your attitude, reflexes, and perceptions—and those of your line handlers. These components of docking situations combine in patterns of infinite variety. Learning them individually, and then in concert, will give you a foundation of experience that can enable you to deal with the difficult and unexpected.

Throughout all the maneuvers described in this book, you are urged to keep your speed to a minimum. I don't mean that you should always operate at slow speed, because conditions sometimes call for a fast approach and sudden stop to safely reach the dock. What I do urge is that you use only enough power to handle the situation and realize that most situations can be handled at slow speed.

The instructions given here are meant as a guide to help you build skills and develop plans for various docking situations. They are not meant to be taken as rules. In each case, you must decide if the actions you're taking are having the desired effect. If not, then you alone must choose an alternative. Your maneuvers should always be guided by safety, courtesy, and adherence to the Navigation Rules.

It makes good sense to start your practice of docking and undocking on a calm, quiet day. Choose a berth at the end of an uncrowded dock with a clear approach. Leave enough room to turn away easily if you make a mistake. Once you do it right, do it again so you'll remember how it feels.

After you've mastered the maneuver on a calm day, do it again when there's a breeze. Pick an empty dock so that you approach into the wind, then find another one where you'll be set off (pushed away from the dock), and so on, until you feel comfortable in all situations. Only by practice will you develop proper timing and technique.

Many people consider good dockmanship to be the mark of a competent skipper. It certainly is the part of boat handling that is most visible to others. It's also a subject that has fascinated me since the beginning of my nautical career. In travels on a variety of yachts, tugs, research vessels, and sailing ships, I've seen the best and worst of it and discovered that many other captains, pilots, and boat operators also find maneuvering in close quarters the most challenging and satisfying part of their job. Some have even achieved a docking nirvana and will do nothing else, turning things over to their mates as soon as the channel is made and not putting their hand in again until the pier is in sight.

This fascination has inspired me to teach promising mates and deckhands, lead docking seminars for sailing clubs, spend many hours with kindred spirits maneuvering matchbooks alongside cocktail napkins, and write this book.

Dockmanship

1. The Basics

PROPELLER

Each make and model of boat has its own handling characteristics. Responses to wind and current vary from one boat to another, and, even among like models, may differ according to distribution of weight, hull condition, and the presence of optional wind-catching accessories.

Two of the major docking tools you'll have to master are the engine and the rudder. Different types of engines and rudders cause boats to respond in different ways. Once you understand how they work on *your* boat, the good news is that these responses are predictable and won't change from day to day.

Standing astern (behind the boat) and looking forward, port side is on the left and starboard is on the right. Port and starboard are the same whichever way you face and however the boat moves.

Propellers are named according to their direction of rotation. Viewed from astern, a right-handed propeller turns clockwise when engaged in forward gear and counterclockwise when put in reverse. A left-handed propeller does the opposite. You can determine which way your propeller turns by looking at the engine. In many cases, the flywheel housing at the front of the engine has an arrow indicating direction of rotation in forward. If you face aft toward the front of an engine that turns counterclockwise, you have a left-handed engine and a right-handed prop. You may also be able to observe a short length of the shaft where it comes out of the gearbox. With the engine in forward at minimal throttle you can see which way the shaft turns. If the top of it rotates to starboard, you're dealing with a right-handed prop.

Let's concentrate on the right-handed propeller (RHP) first, since the majority of single-screw inboards are of this type. Left-handed props cause the opposite response. The actions of outboards and inboard/outboards (I/O's) are covered in a later chapter.

Looking down at the propeller (figure 1-1) notice the top blade and how it is angled. If the blades were perpendicular to the shaft, they would slice through the water without any resistance. If they were parallel to the shaft, they would just paddle the stern to one side or the other. Their angle, or pitch, is what pushes water astern and moves the boat forward. When pitched blades spin clockwise, high pressure is built up on the after side and low pressure on the forward side, drawing the boat ahead (figure 1-1). Water drawn into the prop is called suction current. Water spun away is called discharge current or prop wash. Of the two, discharge current is more focused and exerts greater force.

This thrust, which can propel the boat either ahead or astern depending on which way the prop is rotated, has a

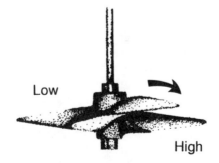

Fig. 1-1

partner called side force. As the right-handed prop turns clockwise, water is spun away to starboard but up against the hull to port. This creates high pressure to port and low pressure to starboard, moving the stern to starboard (figure 1-2). In addition, the angling of the shaft downward toward the propeller end presents more of an angle of blade to the water on the downward (starboard) side and less on the upward (port) side. The result is more thrust on the starboard side which adds to the side force effect of walking the stern to starboard; it's as if you were powering a rowboat with a big oar on the starboard side and a small oar on the port. In some boats, this is countered by offsetting the shaft and propeller to port.

In reverse, the RHP turns counterclockwise and has the opposite effect. Water is drawn from the port side up against the hull to starboard. The resulting high pressure walks the stern to port.

Side force is mostly overcome by the forward motion at cruising speed, but can have considerable effect at low speeds, especially in reverse or when the engine is first engaged and there is little or no way on. Instead of going straight ahead or astern, the back of the boat angles to

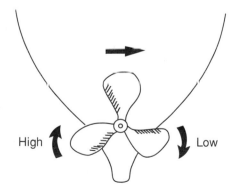

High   Low

Fig. 1-2

starboard in forward and port in reverse. With a left-handed prop, the stern walks to port in forward and to starboard in reverse. The effect varies from boat to boat and ranges from minimal to dramatic, being generally more pronounced in reverse than in forward. Once you determine which way your prop turns, just remember that side force walks the stern in the direction the top blade is moving. With twin-screw inboards, the props rotate in opposite directions, so side forces are cancelled when both engines are in the same gear, and compounded when the engines are in opposite gears. Docking with twin screws is covered in detail in chapter 5.

RUDDER

The rudder also moves the stern from side to side by setting up pressure differentials, but must have water flowing against it to work. Going ahead, when the rudder is turned to starboard, high pressure builds on the leading edge. Low pressure develops on the port side, and the stern moves to port (figure 1-3). Water pressure exerts a force perpendicular to the surface it strikes, so the greater the rudder angle, the sharper the turn. Also, the greater the flow of water past the rudder, the more pronounced the rudder effect. This means that at slow boat speed, steering can be sluggish and at higher speed more responsive.

Placing the rudder behind the propeller puts it in the path of the discharge current when going ahead, This increases the water flow and the rudder's effectiveness. There's no such benefit in going astern because the prop wash is thrown forward, away from the rudder. With headway (forward motion), turning the rudder to one side pushes the stern to the opposite side and so the bow swings to the same side as the rudder.

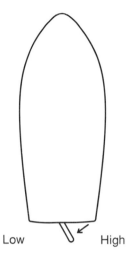

Fig. 1-3   Low   High

On boats steered with a tiller connected directly to the rudder, you put the tiller away from the side you want the bow to turn. With wheel steering, you turn the top of the wheel in the direction you want the bow to move, and a system (usually cables) turns the rudder to that side. Turning the top of the wheel to the right causes "right rudder," which turns the bow to starboard. "Left rudder" has the opposite effect. Rudder is left, right, or amidships, that is, steering the boat to port, starboard, or straight, respectively. In reverse, turning the rudder to one side moves the stern to that same side. Left rudder backs you to port, right rudder, to starboard.

In forward, putting the rudder over actually swings the stern out, causing the boat to turn slightly angled rather than along a neat line (figure 1-4). The boat turns on a pivot point about one-third of the way back with the bow following a tighter circle than the stern. Remember this when trying to get off a dock: turning the bow away from

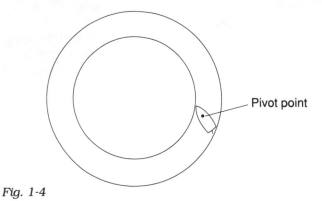

Pivot point

Fig. 1-4

the dock brings the stern towards it, so make sure you're clear before putting the rudder over. In reverse, with the rudder over, the bow swings way out, describing a larger circle than the stern, and the pivot point is much farther aft, near the rudderpost or stern of the boat. The pivot point is the spot along its centerline on which a boat turns; it varies from boat to boat and is something you must observe for yourself.

Some boats have "balanced rudders," that is, they have up to one-quarter of the area of the rudder forward of the rudderpost. This takes some strain off the steering system and makes the boat easier to handle.

Starting from dead in the water (no way on) and in neutral, the rudder has no effect because there is no water flowing past it. Putting the engine ahead, the side force of a right-handed prop may kick the stern to starboard. This can be corrected with some right rudder even before you gain headway since the discharge current acts on the rudder immediately. In forward, the effect of discharge current is so much greater than that of side force that you should always check the rudder position before going ahead. Once you have headway, right rudder turns the bow to starboard, left rudder turns it to port. When you reduce engine speed to idle, the boat is still steerable as long as you have headway. As you drift to a stop, all steering is lost. Putting the engine in reverse won't give you steering until you develop sternway and have water flowing past the rudder again. Reversing with a right-handed propeller will quickly start to walk the stern to port. Once you have sternway, left rudder turns the stern sharply to port, rudder amidships backs you moderately to port, and right rudder backs you straight or slightly to starboard, depending on the extent of the side force. If you engage reverse while coasting forward, side force pulls the stern to port, but you can keep the boat straight with a little left rudder. As long as you have headway, the boat will respond to forward steering no matter what gear you employ, and even when you're stopped or backing, an application of forward power will turn the bow toward the rudder by directing prop wash against it.

WIND AND CURRENT

Wind acts on the part of the vessel above the waterline. On most, but not all boats, the bow presents the greatest surface area to the wind, so is most affected by it.

Current acts on the part of the vessel below the waterline. A shallow-draft planing hull is more affected by wind than it is by current. A full-keeled boat with low freeboard is more easily moved by current than it is by wind.

Some boats sit broadside to the wind or current, others point away. To see how yours behaves, stop in open water and allow the boat to drift. Knowing how your boat responds to wind and current is vital to safe and successful operation.

In most docking situations, wind will be the major factor, although current, if present, must not be ignored. The effects of wind are more completely described in the following chapters, but, in general, the responses one would make should apply as well in situations where current is the dominant force. However, it may be necessary to modify your approach, maneuvering, and line handling depending on how your boat is affected by current.

When both wind and current are present, their net effect must be determined. This can be done before reaching the dock by stopping your boat or observing other boats at anchor.

SUMMARY

—Right-handed prop kicks the stern to starboard in forward, to port in reverse.

—Left-handed prop kicks the stern to port in forward, to starboard in reverse.

—With headway, right rudder turns the bow to starboard, left rudder takes it to port. The sharper the rudder angle, the tighter the turn.

—With sternway, right rudder backs the stern to starboard, left rudder backs it to port.

2. Lines and Fenders

Lines and fenders play crucial roles in successful dock-manship. Even the best docking maneuver won't do you or your boat any good unless the dock lines are quickly and properly employed to secure the boat in place, and fenders are positioned to protect it from floats and pilings.

DOCK LINES

For proper boat handling, you should have enough lines of sufficient length and diameter to secure the boat in all conditions you expect to encounter. For a thirty-foot boat, half-inch three-strand or braided nylon line is recommended, and you should have at least one fifty-foot and four thirty-foot lengths. At one end each line should have an eye splice or bowline large enough to fit over a piling. The other end should be whipped or burned to keep the end strands from unraveling. Lines that are not in use should be coiled and stowed out of sunlight and free from dirt, grease, or paint.

A line is belayed to a cleat by taking one round turn around the base of the cleat (figure 2-1), then three figure-eight turns around the horns. This should be enough to hold any strain. To make the line fast, use two and a half turns plus a locking hitch (formed by twisting the line half a turn so it passes under itself).

Fewer turns may not hold—and topping too few turns with a locking hitch may cause the line to jam under a strain. If you are using the right diameter line and can't get three turns around a cleat, then the cleat is probably too small for the boat. The line should be led to the cleat as shown in figure 2-1, not as in figure 2-2. Correctly leading the line enables you to ease, check, and surge it without jamming, and also minimizes wear from friction.

Never finish taking turns around a cleat with the part of the line that is to take the strain on top. This should be the first part turned around the cleat so that the final top turns are not under strain. Then the line can be easily cast off or eased under control.

If you are using the looped end of the line rather than the bitter end, it can be secured to a cleat by passing the bight through the hole in the base, entering from the side the line will lead toward when it takes a strain. Then open the loop, put it over both horns, and take up the slack by pulling on the standing part of the line (figure 2-3).

The loop may also be placed on a cleat by just putting it over both horns (figure 2-4). This will not be quite as secure, especially if the line leads up from the cleat. The looped end is normally secured to a piling by simply placing it over the top of the piling. If the loop isn't large enough, then reach through it, grab the standing part of the line, and pull it back through the loop to make a slip loop (figure 2-5).

Fig. 2-1

Fig. 2-2

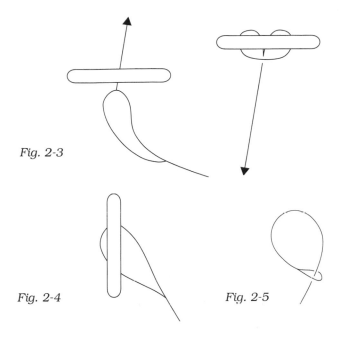

Fig. 2-3

Fig. 2-4   Fig. 2-5

If another line is already on the piling, then your loop should be brought up through the first loop before being placed over the piling (figure 2-6). This is called "dipping a line," and allows either line to be removed without disturbing the other. Lines on a cleat may be dipped if they are looped as shown in figure 2-4.

Some people secure the looped end of their line on board and send the other end ashore to be tended. This can work well for smaller boats that are easily pulled around by one person on the pier. As the boat comes alongside, a crew member can step ashore with a line ready to be made off to a cleat or piling on the dock.

On larger boats, however, it is more common to put the looped end ashore and tend the line from on board. In this

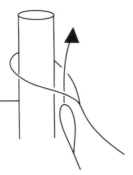

Fig. 2-6

case, a crew member will either step ashore with the eye of the line or toss it to someone on the dock. One advantage to this method is that it makes it easier for you to maintain control.

Anytime you hand over a line to someone on the dock, make sure it is placed where you want it, not where he or she thinks it should go. Complete strangers will literally take over your boat if you let them, directing you and your crew in every aspect of the maneuver. Don't let them.

Contrary to popular usage, the clove hitch (figure 2-7, left) is not the best choice for making a line fast to a piling. A clove hitch should never be trusted as being fully secure, since under a strain, it can first slip then jam, making it

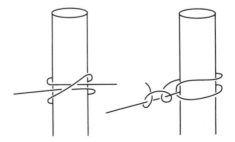

Fig. 2-7

difficult to adjust or undo, even on a temporary tie-up. To make a line fast to a piling, try the hitch shown in figure 2-7, right. It's quick to tie, secure under a strain, and easy to surge or untie after taking a strain.

Line handling has its own vocabulary. The following terms apply when one end of the line is on board and the other is ashore:

Slack—feed line out.

Take up—take slack out.

Ease—pay out line as the boat moves.

Check—as you ease a line, hold it intermittently to slow a moving boat.

Hold—have enough turns around a cleat to control a line under tension and keep the boat stopped, but still be ready for further maneuvering.

Surge—momentarily ease a line under strain to let a stopped boat move.

Make fast—secure the line.

All fast—secure all lines; the maneuver is finished.

Double up (the bow)—put out a second (bow) line.

And, in addition, when undocking:

Single up—take off doubled lines in preparation for getting underway.

Stand by the (after-leading spring) line—take the (after-leading spring) line in hand and be ready to tend it.

Let go—cast off.

It is important that you and your crew understand and use these terms so that your intentions are not misunderstood.

Sometimes it is not possible to get the boat close enough to the dock for a crew member to step ashore with a line. This is often the case when a strong wind sets the boat off. The line can be thrown, however, if there's someone ashore to catch it. To do so properly, prepare enough line to reach the dock in clockwise coils about two feet in diameter. Hold three or four loops in your throwing hand and the rest in the other hand. The throw should be made side-armed, starting from behind you with good follow-through. Let the momentum of the toss take the remaining coils from the other hand. If the eye of the looped end is held open, you may even be able to land it around a cleat or piling.

When the distance to be covered is considerable, a heaving line is used. This is a line forty to a hundred feet long, about one-quarter inch in diameter, with one end woven into a monkey's fist to concentrate its weight (figure 2-8). The other end is tied to the loop of the dock line. The heaving line can be tossed as described above from the part of the boat closest to the dock regardless of where the dock line will be made off. Whoever catches it pulls it ashore, along with one end of your dock line.

Fig. 2-8

Getting underway, crew members usually take the lines off the pilings and bring them aboard. If one line is held to maneuver the boat, and there is no one ashore to cast it off, conditions may make it difficult for your crew to do it and get back on board safely. In this case, both ends of the line can be held on board with a large bight passed around the cleat or piling on the dock (figure 2-9).

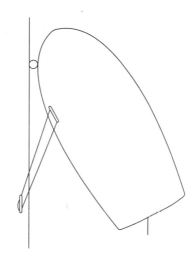

Fig. 2-9

While the line is under strain, both ends are fast to the cleat on the boat. To retrieve the line, cast off one end and pull on the other part until it is all on board. This is called "doubling," not to be confused with "doubling up." Be careful that the line can't snag anything on the dock as it is pulled off and that it doesn't get fouled in your prop while it's in the water.

It takes practice, but it's not too hard to learn to flip a line off a piling with an upward snap of the wrist. Casting a line off a cleat this way takes a little more skill: you must combine a sideways and upward motion. For the less dexterous, a boathook can add several feet to your reach.

Standard dock lines for alongside mooring are shown in figure 2-10: A, bow line; B, forward-leading spring line; C, after-leading spring line; and D, stern line. Spring lines are named for the direction they go once they leave the boat. Breast lines, which run perpendicularly from boat to dock, may also be used.

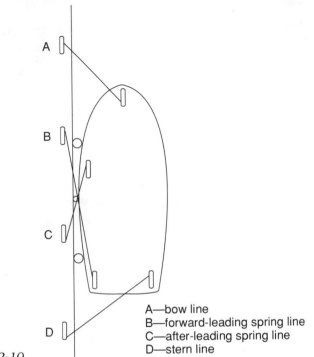

A—bow line
B—forward-leading spring line
C—after-leading spring line
D—stern line

Fig. 2-10

Lines are normally set so that the boat sits parallel to the dock. When possible, any strain should be shared by at least two lines. For example, bow and forward-leading spring lines would do the work while stern and after-leading spring lines are slack if there's wind or current on the bow. There should be enough slack to account for tide, and where it is extreme, lines may have to be tended at various stages.

In moderate to strong wind, the boat may not sit quietly alongside, but rather be quite lively, causing dock lines to

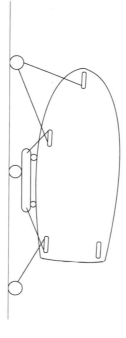

Fig. 2-11

chafe against sharp corners on piers or deck fittings. A line can be cut through quickly unless chafing gear is in place to protect it. This can be made from a length of hose, canvas, or cloth wrapped around the line and secured by twine.

If wind or current is strong, you probably should double up on the line taking the most strain. In a head wind, this means putting out a second bow line and adjusting it to share the load with the first one. It can be led to a separate cleat or piling, especially if dockside fittings are of questionable strength. Preparing to get underway, you'd take off any doubled lines, or single up.

FENDERS

Fenders are used to protect the boat from wear or bangs against docks and pilings. They are made of rubber, plastic, or rope and should have a length of line to secure them to either boat or dock. They may be tied off horizontally or vertically and should be thoughtfully placed to provide maximum protection (figure 2-10). If the fenders are hung from the boat vertically, a board may be tied off on the boat and placed against them to bear on a piling (figure 2-11, preceding page).

As you will see in the following chapters, lines and fenders are not just for holding a boat snugly in place. Properly used, they play an active and creative role in dockmanship, working in harmony with rudder and engine.

3. Handling a Boat with an
Inboard Engine

Right-handed propellers are the most common single-screw type. They set the stern to starboard when put ahead and kick it to port when reversed. Left-handed props have the opposite effect.

PORT SIDE TO

In a Calm. To illustrate the basic docking maneuver, we'll consider a boat with RHP, port side to on a calm day. In general, the approach should be made slowly, but with enough speed to maintain steerage. This treats your machinery gently, gives you time to assess your progress and make adjustments, and minimizes or prevents damage if you hit something.

Come in at a 15- to 25-degree angle to the dock (figure 3-1). Try to maintain this angle throughout the approach. As you draw near, you can take the engine out of gear to slow down. Approach with the throttle low—then forget it and try using only the gear shift. Apply forward, neutral, or reverse as necessary. This gives you one less control to worry about. If you lose momentum too soon, shift to forward just long enough to regain it. Remember though, an RHP may kick the stern to starboard (bow to port) when first engaged ahead. You can correct this with right rudder.

When the bow is about five feet off, reverse the engine and put the rudder away from the dock (in this case, to

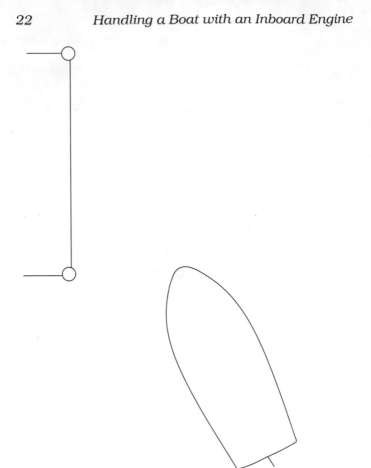

Fig. 3-1

starboard). The rudder will straighten you out—reversing
will kick the stern to port and stop the boat. If you find
that you need more throttle in reverse to come to a
complete stop, apply it smoothly, and don't forget to
throttle down and shift to neutral before you gain sternway.

Notice what happens when the engine is reversed while you still have forward way on. The stern kicks to port even though you are moving ahead, and the rudder responds normally even though you are in reverse. Once you lose way, the rudder is ineffective and the stern will continue its walk to port. Then, as you develop sternway, the rudder can be used again, but side force is still present.

As the boat stops, the after-leading spring line is passed ashore. If you have someone on board to handle lines, send the looped end ashore to go around a cleat or piling, and tend the line from on board. Get all slack out of the line and take a couple of turns around the cleat. By putting the engine ahead with minimal power you can now hold the boat against the dock. If the boat isn't parallel to the dock, bring the bow in with left rudder or the stern in with right rudder. Fenders should be in place to cushion the boat and give it points on which to pivot when maneuvering alongside. Once in position, get bow, stern, and forward-leading spring lines on and secured.

All things being equal, it is preferable to dock a single engine RHP boat port side to because the stern walks toward the dock when you go into reverse. A left-handed prop behaves the opposite way. Going ahead from dead in the water walks the stern to port (bow to starboard). Putting the engine in reverse kicks the stern to starboard. Docking a boat with LHP starboard side to is like docking a boat with RHP port side to—in each case, the stern comes in for an easy landing.

Now we will consider docking in wind and current. Unless otherwise stated, directions such as "on the bow" or "on the beam" are relative to the boat when it is alongside, regardless of the approach angle. "On the bow" and "on the stern" are roughly parallel to the dock, "setting on" and "setting off" are perpendicular to it.

On the Bow. With wind or current on the bow, or nearly so, you have to employ a little more power to maintain the same speed and steerageway than you would on a calm day. Approach at a 15- to 25-degree angle, but guard against wind or current catching the bow and forcing it to one side or the other when you have little or no headway.

Throttle down and shift to neutral to stop, using reverse only as necessary. Pass the after-leading spring ashore, take slack out, then come ahead slow against it. If the bow is set slightly on the dock, put your rudder away to work the stern in, and get the stern line on next (figure 3-2). If the bow is set off, put the rudder toward the dock and secure the bow line, then the stern and forward-leading spring before coming out of gear.

As wind or current become stronger, you need even more power to maintain steerageway, but it's easy to stop. Just throttling back or going to neutral should do the job. When you don't use reverse, there's no side force to throw the stern over.

Setting Off. When the wind or current is anywhere from broad on the bow to broad on the quarter and setting off the dock, you must approach faster and at a greater angle to overcome it. This shouldn't be too difficult if the stern backs toward the dock. More reverse power is required to stop while putting the rudder away from the dock to straighten out.

Use a heaving line if necessary to get an after-leading spring ashore, then come ahead on the spring with rudder toward the dock to bring the bow in (figure 3-3). Get the

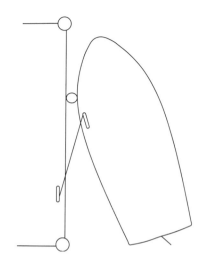

Fig. 3-2

bow line on next, then shift your rudder to bring the stern in.

If the wind is abaft (behind) the beam, you'll need more power in reverse to stop the boat. Once the after-leading spring is on and the boat is stopped, you can come ahead slow against the line and apply rudder away from the dock if needed to bring the stern in first. Get the stern line on, then shift the rudder to bring the bow in. Put the bow line on, then the forward-leading spring.

When the wind is blowing off hard, you may find yourself stopped too far off to get a line ashore. This can easily happen, since the boat is probably being set even before you begin to slow down. Once you slow and stop, the boat (especially the bow) can be blown off very quickly. If this happens and you don't have enough room to leeward to turn and approach again, just back slowly to the dock. This works especially well if the wind is abaft the beam.

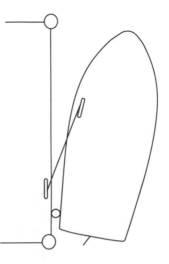

Fig. 3-3

Be sure the water is deep enough and the area around the pier is clear of hazards that may damage the steering or propulsion systems.

Your boat will readily back into the wind under control. Once stern to, put a line ashore and lead it to the middle cleat. Take all slack out, then come ahead with the rudder toward the dock. Have a fender in place aft to cushion the boat and help it pivot (figure 3-4). You may need to surge the line a bit to get the boat turning. Once you've swung around parallel to the dock on this after-leading spring, set the bow line, then the stern line and the forward-leading spring.

Setting On. Being set on the dock requires that you approach more from windward and not have any way on when you reach it. Stop a boat width or more off the dock, not quite parallel to it, but with the bow inclined a point or so to windward. Then just drift, applying short bursts

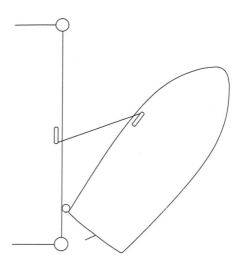

Fig. 3-4

of forward or reverse to keep positioned and angled correctly. Have fenders in place before you land.

Moving the boat along a dock while you're pinned against it can cause damage. That's why you should be in position with neither headway nor sternway when dock and boat touch. Once alongside, the wind will hold the boat against the dock bow in. Put an after-leading spring on, take slack out, hold the line, and apply forward with the rudder away from the dock to bring the stern in (figure 3-2). Secure the stern line, then the bow line and the forward-leading spring line.

On the Stern. An upwind landing is preferable to a downwind one. The headwind or current helps stop you and allows slow speed and greater control. A tailwind or current makes it harder to approach slowly and stop.

If you must make a downwind landing, come in fairly straight and slow the boat well before you near the dock, using as much reverse as necessary. Apply short bursts ahead only if you need them to steer. In strong winds, be sure that you can control the boat and stop it before you attempt the maneuver.

Putting an after-leading spring line on first may trip the bow into the dock and send the stern out, especially if the wind catches the stern. With a moderate to strong wind, it can be difficult to straighten out once this has happened. In this case, get the stern line on first and be ready to ease and check it until all way is off. Once the boat is stopped and the stern line made fast, a little forward power with the rudder toward the dock should bring the bow in. If not, you'll need an after-leading spring to hold and pivot the boat while you slowly ease the stern line. Bow line and forward-leading spring are attached next.

The above examples for RHP port side to also apply to LHP starboard side to. Just exchange left and right in rudder directions and side force.

STARBOARD SIDE TO

Docking starboard side to with RHP can be awkward if the boat displays significant side force. Reversing the engine pulls the stern away from the dock so that you end up angled to it. This also applies to LHP port side to.

In a Calm. Approach at a shallow angle (about 15 to 20 degrees) as slowly as possible in order to minimize the need for reverse (figure 3-5). The less reverse power you use, the less the stern will be pulled away from the dock by side force.

As long as you still have headway when you engage reverse, putting the rudder away from the dock (to port) will help keep you parallel to the dock, but both bow and

Fig. 3-5

stern will now be farther away from it. Have a long line ready and someone standing by to catch it. Once an after-leading spring line is on, come ahead slowly with left rudder to bring the stern in (figure 3-6). Make the stern line fast, then shift the rudder if necessary to bring the

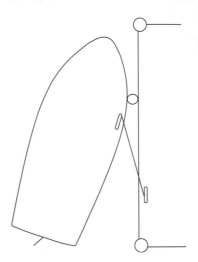

Fig. 3-6

bow in. Secure the bow and forward-leading spring, then take the engine out of gear.

On the Bow. Here you have the advantage of being stopped by the wind, so there should be little or no need for reverse, which would pull the stern away from the dock. Approach as above, but guard against the port bow being caught by the wind and set on the dock as you lose headway.

Use only enough speed to maintain steerageway. Shift to neutral so that the boat will just about drift to a stop. With the bow about five feet off, turn the rudder away and gently reverse if necessary to stop. Get the after-leading spring on, slack out, and come ahead slow to position the boat. The bow line goes on next, followed by the stern line. If required, use right rudder to bring in the bow, left rudder to bring in the stern. Once the forward-leading spring is on, take the engine out of gear and see how the boat sits.

Setting Off. Wind blowing off the dock makes RHP starboard landings more difficult. This situation requires a greater approach angle so that the stern is canted away from the dock from the start, and the increased forward speed needed to overcome leeway demands more reverse power to stop. The accompanying increase in side force turns the stern even farther out.

If the wind is forward of the beam, steer close to it and come in as slowly as possible to decrease the need for reverse. When the bow is close to the dock, turn the rudder away, go to neutral, and reverse only if necessary. The wind should catch the bow and help push it off. Get the after-leading spring on first to work yourself in with engine ahead slow and right rudder (figure 3-7), then get the bow line on to hold the bow.

If the wind is aft of the beam, consider docking the other way around, so that the wind is on the bow and the engine backs your stern toward the dock instead of away from it.

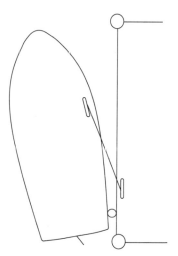

Fig. 3-7

Otherwise, decrease the angle of attack and start your approach farther upwind. Plan to drift with the wind instead of powering to overcome it. Minimize the need for reverse, which would pull your stern away from the dock. With the wind on the quarter, you'll probably be coming in a bit faster than you'd like to.

If you put an after-leading spring line on first, be careful that it doesn't take any strain while you still have headway. With the full reverse needed to make a downwind landing, the rudder won't be able to overcome the side force as you slow down. Not only will the stern swing out, but the line may trip the bow into the dock.

It may be better to get the stern line on first to hold the stern near the dock and the boat fairly parallel to it. Once you're completely stopped, get an after-leading spring line on and come ahead on it slowly with the rudder toward the dock if necessary to bring the bow in. Ease the stern line as you go.

Setting On. When the wind sets you on, the bow is blown toward the dock. Reversing pulls the stern away, compounding the condition.

In this case, approach fairly parallel to the dock, about two boat widths off. As you slow, angle the bow onc to two points to windward and let yourself get set downwind. Make sure there is neither headway nor sternway when boat and dock meet. If the boat isn't parallel when this happens, don't try to use the engine to straighten out at the last minute. As long as the fenders are in place, being angled is preferable to having way on when you hit.

Remember that using reverse will pull the stern away from the dock and send the bow toward it. Once the bow starts swinging this way, the wind will compound the effect.

On the Stern. As in a port side downwind landing, come in straight and as slow as possible. Use as much reverse as necessary to allow you to stop the boat, and apply short bursts ahead only as you need them to straighten the approach. Since reversing pulls the stern away from the dock, you won't want an after-leading spring right away. If the wind catches the stern and you still have a little headway while reversing, the bow will surely get tripped into the dock by this line.

The stern line is the first line to put ashore, but if the stern comes away from the dock as you stop, you may not be able to reach the dock with your line. In this case, the bow may be closer to the dock, so have a line ready forward, send it ashore, and quickly walk it aft to the stern as you come to a stop. Once this line is held, use it or an after-leading spring line to work yourself alongside and get bow and forward-leading spring lines on.

The above section applies to LHP port side to by reversing left and right rudder commands and port and starboard side forces.

GETTING AWAY

The first thing to do before getting underway is to decide on a plan. Notice whether you are being pinned against the dock or set off it. Determine which lines are under strain and which are slack. Check around pilings for signs of current, and test the engine in forward and reverse. Lines that are slack can be taken off to simplify the maneuver.

It's generally better to motor a boat off a dock stern first than bow first. Since the stern has greater draft and houses prop and shaft, it should be kept clear of docks and shallows if possible. RHP vessels starboard side to will effortlessly back away from the dock, as will LHP's port side to. RHP port side to must be coaxed out. Put a fender in place forward, and come ahead on the after-leading spring after taking off all other lines. Put the rudder hard toward the dock to bring the bow in and stern out. Once the stern is out far enough, reverse the engine, shift the rudder, and back away.

On the Bow. When you have a headwind or current, let it take the bow away from the dock, then come ahead. If you try to back off, the bow may get set against the dock and bounced from piling to piling as you back. You can put fenders aft, then back on the forward-leading spring to work the bow out.

Setting Off. Getting set off the dock, you can just cast off your lines and back out if the stern backs away from the dock. If the stern backs toward the dock, it's best to cast off all lines, let the wind take you off a bit, then go ahead.

Remember that the pivot point of the boat is well ahead of the rudder. As the bow is turned away, the stern is turned in. Be sure that the stern will clear the dock before you apply any rudder to your forward motion, then do so gradually. Once the stern begins to come away, rudder angle can be increased. If you have no way on and the bow is well out, you can turn the rudder toward the dock and use a short burst of forward power to kick the stern out. This will, of course, bring the bow in a bit as well. Backing away from the dock also calls for the gradual application of rudder so as not to swing the bow into it.

Setting On. Being set on the dock isn't too bad if your stern backs away from it. Come ahead on the after-leading spring line, with the rudder toward the dock until the stern is as far out as you can get it, then back smartly and shift the rudder.

When you're being set on the dock, an engine that backs toward it will only rake you along the pilings, even if you try kicking the stern out first. Alternatives are warping and anchor techniques decribed in chapter 8, or simply planning ahead by docking your RHP boat starboard side to (LHP port side to) if you think you'll be getting underway when the wind is setting on.

On the Stern. Single-screw boats love to back to windward, so cast off bow and spring lines, and, as you slowly start to back away, cast off the stern line. With a firm hand on the wheel or tiller, apply slight rudder to bring yourself gradually away from the dock.

TURNING

To turn around in a narrow channel or other confined area you must cast (turn in place) by working alternately ahead and astern. It's easiest to short turn RHP vessels to starboard (clockwise) because they back to port.

With full right rudder, come ahead, then back with moderate throttle, and the side force will keep you turning. There's no need to shift the rudder unless you develop sternway. When your turn starts losing momentum, shift to forward. The rudder should still be to starboard and will help continue the turn. Reverse again if necessary, and so on, until the turn is completed. LHP boats cast more readily to port (counterclockwise).

4. Handling a Boat with an Outboard Motor

Outboard propulsion ranges from low-horsepower electric motors to powerful high-performance stern drives that combine the greater power capability of an inboard with the more responsive direct-thrust steering of an outboard. Also known as inboard/outboards or outdrives, stern drives are included under the outboard heading here since, for docking purposes, they behave in the same basic way as outboards.

Outboards differ from inboard engines in that they have no rudder; rather, they depend on the directed thrust of the discharge current to steer the boat because the propulsion unit itself is turned either by tiller or wheel. There's virtually no steerage unless the prop is spinning, so coasting to slow or stop must be done carefully.

The small props produce little side force. Also, since they're almost always placed aft of the transom, water pressure doesn't build against the hull—so the act of changing gears in itself does not throw the stern over.

Because the force of the prop's thrust is aft of the transom, the boat turns sharply around its pivot point—usually about a third of the boat length aft of the bow. When the prop is engaged in forward and directed toward one side, the stern moves toward the other side. When the prop is reversed and directed toward one side, the stern moves toward that side.

Except as auxiliary power for sailboats, outboards are most often found on planing rather than displacement hulls. Since relatively little of the hull is below water, these boats gain and lose way quickly and are more affected by wind than current.

Boats powered by a single outboard engine are usually small and lightweight. Their trim is more easily altered by unequal weight distribution, and this can have a direct bearing on boat handling. A boat down by the bow will have its pivot point farther forward. Being down by the stern moves it aft. Having more weight on one side will make the boat favor turns to that side. Changing the distribution of weight clearly can change the way a small boat behaves. Although these factors are functions of hull type, not propulsion, they are often important considerations when handling outboard-powered boats.

ALONGSIDE

In a Calm. The approach should be made as slowly as possible, using only enough speed to maintain steerage. Come in at a 20- to 25-degree angle to the dock rather than parallel to it (figure 4-1). Approaching parallel to the dock means that any course correction will either bring you into the dock or away from it, whereas approaching at a reasonable angle gives you room to correct yet still maintain the same general attitude with respect to the landing.

Try to maintain the same angle throughout the approach and when the bow is about half a boat length away, turn the propeller away from the dock to bring the bow off. If you have wheel steering, you'll turn the wheel away. If your outboard is steered by a tiller, pulling the tiller toward the dock will have the desired effect.

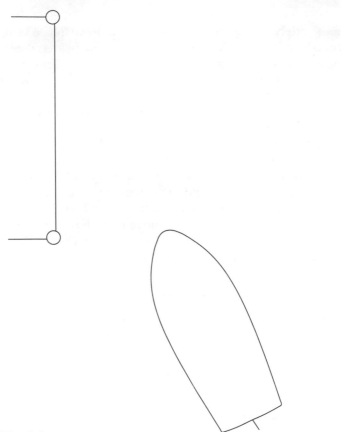

Fig. 4-1

As the bow starts to come off, shift to neutral. Reverse to stop the boat, turning the propeller toward the dock to bring the stern in. Shift to neutral again as the boat comes to rest alongside.

Assuming you've done all this correctly and there's no wind or current to push the boat around, it doesn't make a lot of difference which line goes on first. If there's a cleat amidships or a little forward of it, run an after-leading spring. With a strain on this line, minimal forward power against it will hold the boat snugly alongside. Turn the wheel toward the dock to bring in the bow, away from it to bring in the stern. Bow, stern, and forward-leading spring lines are applied in turn.

Working a boat alongside against an after-leading spring is best done from a midship cleat. If the line is held on a cleat too far forward, the bow gets tripped into the dock—if held too far aft, the bow won't come in. If you don't have a cleat that can take a working spring line, run bow and stern lines first, then spring lines aft from the bow and forward from the stern. In this case, the after-leading spring is not used to control the boat, but along with the forward-leading spring, to keep it secured. Spring lines may be used to work a boat off a dock as explained later in the chapter. Some operators prefer to get a stern line out first for convenience, if that is where the engine and steering controls are and the stern is about the same height as the dock.

On the Bow. When wind or current is roughly parallel to the dock, the favored approach is to put the bow into it. This gives greater control by using the force of nature to both work against and help stop the boat.

Approach generally into the wind, but not at less than a ten-degree angle to the dock, otherwise you may get set into it or away from it before you have a chance to correct.

You should have just enough speed to maintain control. Be careful not to go so slowly that the wind can catch the bow and turn it. As the bow becomes a little less than half a boat length off, turn the wheel away from the dock. If the wind is setting slightly on the dock, turn sooner—if it sets off, turn a bit later.

Put the engine in neutral, then use a touch of reverse if needed to stop. The prop can now be directed toward the dock to bring the stern in. If you run an after-leading spring line, you can put it ashore first and secure it as you would in a calm. If not, then get the bow line out first, followed by stern, forward-leading, and after-leading spring lines.

Setting Off. Approach at a greater angle to the dock (figure 4-2) with the wind just on the bow of the side that will be against the dock. Use enough power to overcome the wind. A moderate to strong breeze will require a faster approach than normal which will have to be held longer than normal.

The greater the angle of approach, the sooner the bow must be turned away. Once it is, the boat should be stopped quickly with as much reverse as necessary. As the boat begins to stop, it will start drifting away from the dock, usually bow first.

If the wind is forward of the beam, either the bow line or after-leading spring should go on first. Take a gradual forward strain on the spring with the wheel toward the dock to bring in the bow. Stern and forward-leading spring lines follow.

When the wind is abaft the beam, deploy either stern line or after-leading spring line. With a strain on the spring, turn the wheel away from the dock to pull the stern alongside (figure 4-3). Bow and forward-leading spring lines are next.

Setting On. Approach at slow speed parallel to the dock, two to three boat widths off. Have fenders in place. Take the motor out of gear so as to be stopped when your docking place is just forward of the beam. Let the wind set you alongside.

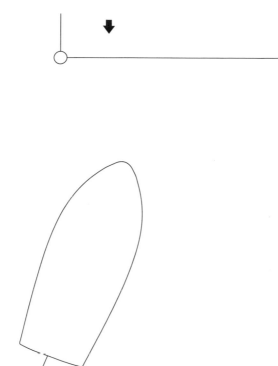

Fig. 4-2

The part of the boat with the greatest above water surface area will be most affected by the wind. Usually this is the bow, so keep it slightly into the wind with the boat angled 10 to 20 degrees away from the dock. Turn the wheel toward the wind shortly before shifting to neutral, and apply short bursts of forward power with the wheel over whenever needed to keep the bow up.

The idea is to be parallel to the dock when you come alongside. Most importantly, carry no way when you hit the dock. Any application of power to correct your angle

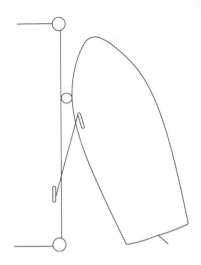

Fig. 4-3

must be made before you near the dock. Close to the dock, a burst of forward with the wheel turned away will bring the stern quickly into the dock. If you have any headway at the moment of impact, you increase the probability of damage.

On the Stern. Downwind landings should be avoided if it is possible to approach bow into the wind. Since it is harder to stop a boat going with wind or current, an element of control is lost and undue strain may be put on the reversing machinery.

If you do dock downwind, approach slowly to keep speed over the bottom to a minimum. Remember, the faster the approach, the more reverse power will be required to stop.

A high, broad transom or superstructure will catch the wind and propel the boat ahead. Shift to neutral or reverse as necessary to keep speed down. Steerage will be lost, so be sure to gear the angle of approach to the wind direction. If it sets slightly on or off the dock, shift your approach a bit to windward. Use forward power only as you need it to steer. A small, low-profile boat will probably be easier to stop in a tailwind, but remember, tidal or wind-generated current may also be at work.

Apply reverse as you near the dock—gradually if your boat has an anti-tilt latch that is not secured, otherwise the prop might kick up out of the water. Turn the wheel toward the dock to bring the stern in as you stop.

The stern line should be first to go ashore. In this case, an after-leading spring would only trip the bow in and allow the stern to swing away from the dock. If not quite all way is off, the stern line can be checked to help stop the boat, but should not be put under too much strain. Don't use dock lines as brakes. The bow or after-leading spring line should go ashore next, followed by a forward-leading spring.

GETTING AWAY

On the Bow. When wind or current is on the bow, set fenders aft, push off forward, and set back on the forward-leading spring until the bow comes off. Come straight ahead slowly, careful not to turn away sharply until the stern is clear of the dock.

If the wind is setting slightly on, you may have to reverse against the forward-leading spring to bring the bow out. The more the bow comes out, the more the stern goes in, so guard against getting the propeller too close to pilings or riprap that might damage it, especially if the lower power unit extends well aft of the transom relative to your boat's beam.

In this case, you can only back so far, but don't attempt to come ahead unless the bow is into the wind or through it. As long as the wind still blows against the outside bow, trying to pull off by going ahead will only rake the stern along the pilings as you attempt to steer away.

Setting Off. When the wind blows off, cast off all lines (usually springs first, then bow and stern), and let the boat drift clear of the dock. Once clear, engage the engine whichever way you want to go.

Setting On. Overcoming wind or current that holds you against a dock can be difficult, although small boats are easier to disengage than larger ones since they are light enough to push off by hand.

In most cases, the safest way of undocking against wind or current is to fender the boat forward, take all slack out of the after-leading spring, and hold it as you gradually increase forward power. Turn the wheel toward the dock, and as the bow comes in, be sure that anchors, railings, stanchions, and the like will not suffer damage against any pilings.

Once the stern is into the wind or as close as it can get, shift to neutral, turn the propeller toward the wind, and back away briskly.

On the Stern. With wind or current on the stern, cast off the stern line last and back away until you are well clear of the dock.

TURNING

To turn a single-screw outboard-powered boat around in close quarters, you must alternately come ahead and back, shifting the wheel each time you shift gears.

To turn clockwise, hold the wheel to the right while in forward. As you start to run out of room ahead, shift to neutral, turn the wheel to the left, then reverse. Repeat this until the turn is complete, using only as much power as you need to do the job. Take advantage of the wind if you can use it to help turn the bow, especially when you have little or no way.

If your boat has trim tabs, they may also be used to facilitate turns in tight places. For example, going ahead to port, try lowering the port tab—backing to starboard, lower the starboard tab. Results will vary from boat to boat, so experiment at very slow speed to find how yours will behave.

5. Handling a Boat with Twin Screws

Two engines give you the versatility and power to handle most docking situations. To understand how they can be used to maneuver a boat, try this on a calm day in open water. Start from dead in the water, and with rudders amidships, engage the starboard engine ahead slow. The boat will turn to port. With both engines ahead, the boat goes straight. Shift the starboard engine to neutral with the port one ahead, and the boat turns to starboard. With just the starboard engine in reverse, the boat backs to port. Both engines astern back it straight, and the port engine alone reversed backs it to starboard.

Just as a twin-screw boat can be steered by shifting engines, it can also be controlled more subtly by varying the throttles when both engines are in the same gear.

The maneuvers described in this chapter apply to twin-screw inboards and outboards alike. Differences between the two types have to do with the presence or lack of side force and rudder, and, where important, will be noted. For an understanding of how these two different engines types behave, review chapter 3 for inboards or chapter 4 for outboards.

With inboard installations, the top propeller blades rotate outward going ahead and inward in reverse. The starboard engine turns a right-handed prop, the port engine a left-handed one. Because the props oppose each other, side forces are cancelled when both are in the same gear. With engines reversed, the starboard prop's pull to port balances the port prop's pull to starboard.

When one engine is in forward and the other is in reverse, side forces are compounded, enabling the boat to turn virtually in place. In addition, with the props off centerline, the twin-screw boat is turned around more efficiently than the single-screw vessel.

For example, when turning the boat counterclockwise with the starboard engine ahead and the port engine reversed, the thrust of the starboard engine turns the bow to port and its side force pulls the stern to starboard. The thrust of the backing port screw also turns the bow to port and its side force pulls the stern to starboard.

For outboard and I/O twin-screw boats, side force isn't a factor in turning, but engine placement off the centerline is. In this respect, all twin-screw boats behave alike. One engine ahead and the other astern will turn the bow toward the backing engine.

Twin-screw inboards, like their single-screw counterparts, have a rudder behind each propeller. It is possible to steer as long as water flows past the rudder(s). With engines ahead and forward way on, steering is at its sharpest because of the prop wash thrown against the rudders in addition to the water flowing past them. With headway and engines in neutral, steering becomes less responsive as you lose way. When engines are reversed, you must develop sternway before you can steer. Responsiveness is again a factor of speed since there's no prop wash to help.

Outboards have no rudders and depend on the direction of their thrust to turn the boat. As soon as you come out of gear on an outboard, you lose steerage, so these boats are reversed to stop rather than coasted to a stop. Once they are put in gear, however, steering is instantaneous.

When speaking of a twin-screw boat alongside or approaching a dock, it is common practice to refer to the engine closest to the dock as the "inboard" one, and the one away as the "outboard." To avoid confusion with these terms as they are used to describe type of propulsion, we'll refer to "inside" or "outside" engines in reference to the side of the boat a particular engine occupies relative to a pier.

ALONGSIDE

The approach should be made with only as much speed as is necessary to control the boat. With two powerful engines to bring you in fast and stop you quickly, the temptation to speed is always present in some people.

A fast approach requires impeccable timing, sharp reflexes, perfect judgment, and infallible equipment. While you may possess some or all of these elements, sooner or later one of them is likely to desert you. It is best not to demand them every time you dock. Some situations require a fast approach and hard stop, but avoid turning every mooring maneuver into such a situation.

In a Calm. Approach at a 15- to 25-degree angle to the dock (figure 5-1). Idle engines as necessary to slow the boat. As the bow nears the dock, back the outside engine and turn the inside one ahead. Adjust throttles as necessary to turn the boat parallel to the dock as it stops. With a ruddered boat, turn the wheel away from the dock as you start backing the outside engine if you require a sharp turn.

As the boat comes to a stop in position, take the engines out of gear and send an after-leading spring line ashore. With all slack out, this line can be held against either engine ahead slow to keep the boat in place. Turn the wheel toward the dock to bring the bow in, away from the dock

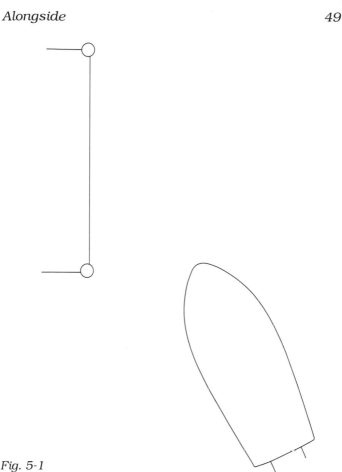

Fig. 5-1

to bring the stern in. Use a fender near the boat's pivot point. Put on bow, stern, and forward-leading spring lines, with fenders in place as needed.

On the Bow. Approach and maneuver as above, but guard against the wind catching the bow as you come to a stop.

You'll need a bit more power to maintain headway, but the wind or current will help you stop.

Hold the boat in place with an after-leading spring line, outside engine ahead, and wheel toward the dock to bring the bow in. Put the bow line on, adjust it until the boat is parallel to the dock, then turn the wheel away from the dock to bring the stern in. After the stern and forward-leading spring lines are on, shift to neutral and see how the boat sets back on the bow and forward-leading spring lines. These two lines should share the strain and the other two should have a little slack in them.

Setting Off. With wind blowing off the dock anywhere from broad on the bow to abeam, approach at a larger angle than before. You should be fairly close to the wind, but keep it just on the side of the bow near the dock (figure 5-2).

As you slow, you'll be set off, so maintain speed and try to hold a constant angle of approach. As the bow nears the dock, slow the inside engine and back the outside one. It shouldn't be necessary to use the wheel because the wind will turn the bow away from the dock.

As you stop in position, get an after-leading spring line on. Fender the pivot point and come ahead slow on the outside engine with the wheel toward the dock to bring the bow in (figure 5-3). Put a bow line out, then shift your wheel to bring the stern in. Once stern and forward-leading spring lines are on, shift to neutral.

Setting On. With fenders in place, approach at a small angle to the dock (10 to 20 degrees) and stop one to two boat widths off by reversing the outside engine and applying forward as necessary on the inside one to cant the bow slightly to windward. The wheel may also be turned away from the dock.

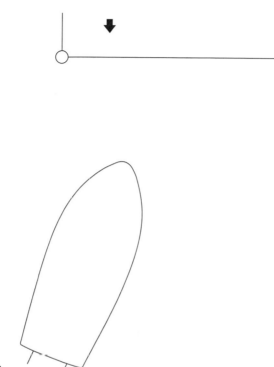

Fig. 5-2

As the wind sets you on, use the engines to keep the bow slightly to windward and the boat in position for its berth. When you reach the dock, the boat should be parallel to it with absolutely no way on.

If the wind is forward of the beam, you'll want an after-leading spring line on first. Come ahead slowly on this line with the wheel turned away from the dock to bring the stern in (figure 5-4). Bow and forward-leading spring lines follow. With wind and current abaft the beam, deploy the stern line first, then spring and bow lines.

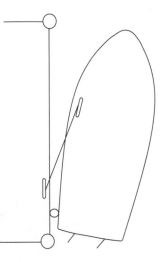

Fig. 5-3

On the Stern. It is usually safer to come alongside bow into the wind or current. With the wind to help stop you, momentum is quickly lost and there is no need to reverse hard. The approach is more controlled and there is less strain on lines and fittings.

If you have no choice but to approach with the wind on the stern, slow the boat well before you reach the dock, especially in moderate to strong conditions. Come in at a 10- to 20-degree angle, as slowly as possible. If the wind is on the inside quarter (blowing slightly off the dock), approach at a smaller angle with the stern more to windward. If the wind is on the outside quarter (setting slightly on), use a larger angle, again with the stern to windward.

As you near the dock, back both engines, increasing power as necessary. You may need more throttle on the outside engine to bring the stern in, or once way is off, put the inside engine ahead slow with rudder away from the dock. With outboards, turn the reversing props toward the

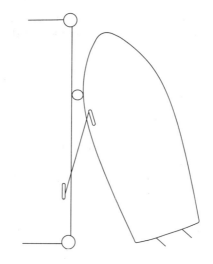

Fig. 5-4

dock to bring the stern in. The first line ashore is the stern line. Using an after leading spring would trip the bow in and the stern out if the line took any strain.

As you stop, throttle down to hold the position. Get the stern line on, then bow and spring lines. Take the engines out of gear and even the tension on the stern and after-leading spring lines.

GETTING AWAY

When deciding whether to come off bow first or stern first, consider wind and current, but also the need to protect the stern from the dangers of shallow water and fouled pilings.

In a Calm. To undock bow first, put the inside engine ahead with rudders amidships. Once clear, put the outside engine ahead. To back out, reverse the inside engine and put the outside one briefly ahead. When clear, reverse both.

On the Bow. Take off stern, after-leading spring, and bow lines. To bring the bow off the dock, gently reverse the outside engine against the forward-leading spring line. Once the wind has the bow, release the line and come ahead on both engines with the rudder straight or slightly toward the dock until the stern clears.

Setting Off. Release springs, then stern and bow lines. As you let yourself get blown off, the bow will come away faster. You may want to put the outside engine ahead with rudder toward the dock or reverse the inside engine if the bow comes off too quickly, then both ahead when clear.

Setting On. Come gently ahead on the outside engine against the after-leading spring line. Back the inside engine to help swing the stern out. Increase power if necessary to do this in a strong wind. Once the stern is angled properly (about 30 to 45 degrees), back smartly on both engines to get away quickly and clear the bow. Rudders should be straight until you're clear.

On the Stern. With the wind coming over the transom, bring the stern out a bit, either by putting the outside engine forward and the inside one in reverse, or by coming ahead on the outside engine against the after-leading spring. Back on both engines until you're away from the dock, then come ahead.

TURNING

Turning a twin-screw boat in place is easily done by putting one engine ahead and the other astern. The bow will turn toward the backing engine, which should be run at higher speed than the forward one.

With no way on, the rudder can be kept amidships. It will have more effect if you have headway, in which case you'd turn it toward the backing screw.

To walk a twin-screw vessel sideways, to starboard, for example, start from dead in the water. With the wheel hard to port, reverse the starboard engine and put the port engine ahead. If the bow comes in too much, shift starboard ahead and port to reverse to bring in the stern.

6. Handling a Boat under Sail

Whether inboard or outboard, auxiliary engines for sail-boats tend to be of relatively low horsepower. With small engines to push very large surface areas through the water, sailboats are slow to start moving but long to carry way. For handling sailboats under auxiliary power, see chapter 3 for inboards, chapter 4 for outboards, and also consider the following.

On V-hull sailboats powered by an inboard engine, side force can be considerable. Water pressure exerts force at right angles to the surface it strikes, so water thrown by the prop against a V-hull will push the hull to the side. Water thrown into a flat-bottom hull will not have this effect, so sailboat hulls usually back to the side more radically than do flatter-bottomed powerboats.

With an outboard for auxiliary power, there's no side force to worry about. When the outboard is mounted on the transom, you don't have the benefit of the discharge current being directed against the rudder. Until sufficient headway is gained, it may be better to steer with the engine. If the outboard is mounted forward of the rudder in a well, then either rudder or engine may be used to steer.

ALONGSIDE

Under sail, rudder action depends solely on the boat's motion through the water since there is no prop wash directed against it. Coasting to a stop may mean losing steerage before you want to. Deep-draft sailboats tend to have less freeboard than draft. The keel resists leeway and holds a boat on course, but also makes it more easily moved by current.

On the Bow. This is generally the easiest and safest way to dock and undock under sail. The following examples illustrate a sloop with jib and mainsail. For docking purposes, wind directions such as "on the bow" and "setting off" are relative to the boat when it is alongside.

Come in close-hauled, luffing as necessary to slow down (figure 6-1). Remember, sailboats are just as slow to lose way as they are to gain it, so leave plenty of stopping room.

Drop the jib several boat lengths off; then as you near the dock, put the rudder away and cast off the mainsheet to keep the sail from catching any wind. Stop with the bow into the wind, roughly parallel to the dock and close enough to get a line ashore. Fenders should be in place forward in case the bow gets set into the dock by the wind. Put a bow line on first, then stern and spring lines.

Setting Off. Approach close hauled (figure 6-2) and luff to keep your speed to a minimum, either by pointing up or by easing sheets. Drop the jib several boat lengths off and come in under main alone. There's no way to tell you here how close to get to the dock before you cast off the mainsheet and turn toward the wind to stop. That depends on wind speed, boat speed, and the boat's stopping characteristics.

The idea is to come to a stop with the wind just off the bow, get a bow line on, and muscle the boat alongside with a second line. It takes skill to stop close enough to send a line ashore without hitting the dock. This must be done with extreme care. It is better to err on the side of caution,

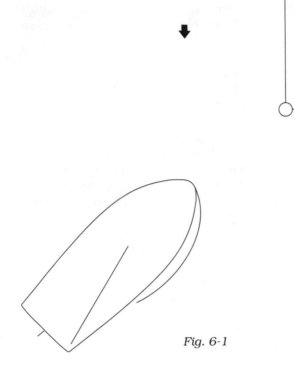

Fig. 6-1

stop short, and try again rather than risk collision. Practice
the maneuver in advance, away from the dock, by approaching a float which you can deploy for this purpose. Attempt
the maneuver only after several successful rehearsals.

Use a heaving line to send the dock lines ashore so that
you don't have to bring the boat in too close. By keeping
the wind just off the bow rather than dead ahead, you keep
the option of turning the boat away if it looks as if you may
hit the dock. Also, if you do hit, it is better to do so at an
angle against fenders than head on.

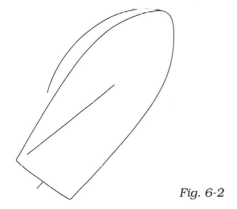

Fig. 6-2

Setting on. This is another difficult maneuver because sails, running rigging, and the main boom all come against the dock before the hull does. To avoid damage, sails must be down and the boom inboard before you settle along-side.

In light air, approach two to three boat widths off, parallel to the dock. The wind should be on the beam or forward of it. Ease sheets to luff the sails and slow the boat. Point 20 to 30 degrees toward the wind, drop the sails, then sheet in the boom. All way should now be off and fenders in place.

The bow is angled out not only to drop the sails, but also because it is the part of the boat that will be set toward the dock soonest. If you've done everything right, the boat will be parallel to the dock when you reach it. Have enough fenders ready forward in case the bow comes alongside first.

This maneuver is not recommended in moderate to strong wind because wind and waves will set you quickly and forcefully against the dock.

What can be done in this situation, and in light airs as well, is to approach parallel to the dock at least one boat length off. Take in the jib, then head up into the wind, sheet in the main, drop it, and once all way is off, let go the anchor.

As the boat is set downwind, pay out rode, then hold it to take a strain and set the anchor. Ease out more anchor line to let the boat drift alongside. Hold the line as needed to keep the boat almost parallel to the dock, bow slightly to windward (figure 6-3).

With fenders in place and the anchor line for control, your landing should be a soft one. Once alongside, bow, stern, and spring lines are made fast. You may keep a strain on the anchor rode to hold the boat off the pilings or dock. If this isn't necessary, then slack it off so as not to impede other boats. In either case, hoist a black ball forward by day and a white light at night to let others know that you have an anchor out.

GETTING AWAY

Setting On. With the wind blowing on the dock, you'll be glad to have an anchor out. Take a strain on the rode, cast off dock lines, and haul away. With the bow into the wind,

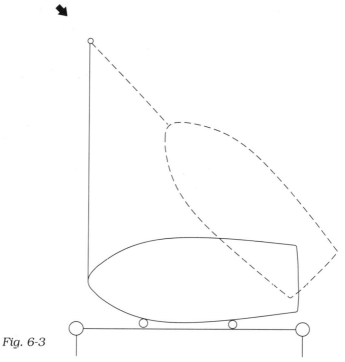

Fig. 6-3

set the main loose-sheeted. As you come up short on the rode, set the jib and be ready to back it.

As the anchor comes off the bottom, hold the clew of the jib to port if you want a port tack, to starboard if that's the tack you desire. Once the bow comes off the wind the way you want it to, sheet in the main, let the jib go over, and sheet it in too.

Setting Off. When the wind blows off, release dock lines and let yourself get set clear. You may either set main and jib or jib alone.

On the Bow. To sail off a dock when the wind is on the bow, release all lines but the forward-leading spring, set the main loose-sheeted, then the jib backed toward the dock (figure 6-4). As the headsail catches the wind, the spring line will take a strain, helping to swing the bow out. Once the bow is far enough out, cast off the spring line, pass the jib to leeward, and sheet in the main.

Neither docking nor undocking under sail with wind or current on the stern is recommended. If you find yourself alongside in this situation when you want to get underway, try casting off all but the bow line, let the stern swing 180 degrees around, and sail off with the wind on the bow as above.

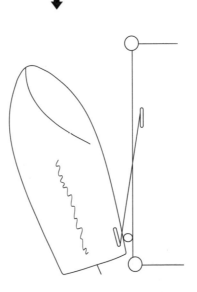

Fig. 6-4

TO A SLIP

Setting Out. Sailing to a slip when the wind blows out is a variation of coming alongside with the wind on the bow. Approach close-hauled and douse the jib before you near the slip. Depending on your speed, point into the wind and the slip when the bow is perhaps a boat length from the outer pilings. The mainsheet should be slack so the sail won't catch any wind. Your momentum should carry the bow partly, but not all the way into the slip so that you coast to a stop and get lines on before hitting anything.

Setting Across. When the wind sets across the slip from either direction, approach close-hauled (figure 6-5). The jib should be dropped when you're several boat lengths off. As the bow nears the outer row of pilings, turn the rudder away (bow into the wind), and cast off the mainsheet. You should coast to a stop alongside the pilings with the stern of the boat at the entrance to the slip.

Put lines on the two outer pilings of your slip, and a long line at the bow, doubled back to the boat so that it can be easily cast off (figure 6-6). These should hold you while you drop the mainsail. Then pull the boat ahead or back as necessary to end up with the stern in front of the slip. Keep a strain on the windward stern line at piling "A," slack off the bow line, and push off at the bow. As the wind catches the bow and swings you around, check the bow line to control the turn, and ease the stern line to allow the boat to back in (figure 6-7).

Work the stern in by pulling on the stern lines as you walk them forward. Once you're at least halfway into the slip, the bow line is cast off and pulled back on board. The lines on the outer pilings are now used to secure the bow, and stern and spring lines are applied as the boat comes all the way into its slip.

Setting In. When the wind blows into the slip, sail to a spot several boat lengths off, douse the jib, head up, and anchor. Ease the anchor rode to let the boat drift back until the stern reaches the outer pilings.

Put lines on that will be walked forward to the bow as the boat is eased back. Once the boat is in place, hold the bow lines, put out stern lines, and slack off the anchor rode.

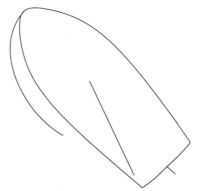

Fig. 6-5

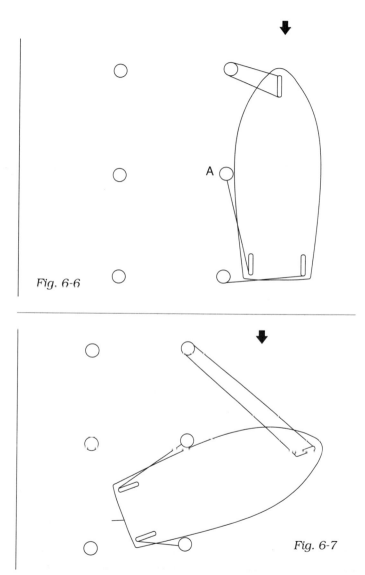

Fig. 6-6

A

Fig. 6-7

7. Getting into a Slip

Depending on whether the wind is setting out, in, or across the slip, backing can be either a simple or difficult maneuver.

In a Calm. With no wind or current to set you, the key to docking a single-screw inboard stern to is gearing your approach to the way the boat backs. With RHP, approach perpendicular to the slip (along the row of outer pilings), keeping it all on your port side. Come in slowly, taking the engine out of gear two or three slips away. Before the bow reaches the slip, turn the rudder away. The boat will turn as long as you have even a little headway. Engage reverse to pull the stern to port and help align the boat with the slip (figure 7-1).

You may need to apply more throttle just long enough to gain sternway. Until then, the rudder will have no effect. Once moving astern, throttle back and turn the wheel the way you want the stern to go.

With twin screws, approach along the pilings from either side. Both engines can be ahead slow and taken out of gear as necessary to slow the boat. As the bow crosses the slip, turn away and back the outside engine while keeping the inside one slow ahead. As the boat aligns with the slip, reverse both engines. As you develop sternway, throttle back and either turn the rudder the way you want the stern to go or keep it amidships and use the engines

66

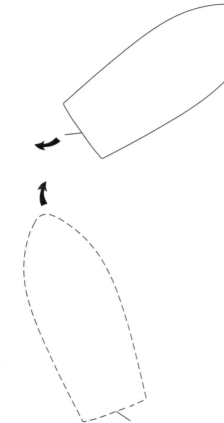

Fig. 7-1

to steer. With either single or twin inboards, the stern can be kicked to one side or the other by a short but firm application of forward power with the rudder away from the side you want the stern to move.

With single or twin outboards, make a similar approach, but since there's no way to steer while in neutral, stay in gear instead of coasting. With just enough throttle to maintain steerageway, turn away as you reach the slip, then engage reverse and steer the boat between the pilings.

Whatever the type of propulsion, there is no need to do this with any great speed in a calm. If you can back straight all the way in, that's fine. If not, just getting the stern between the pilings and coming to a stop will put you in position to get a line or two out and work the boat the rest of the way in. In this case, you should be in neutral before the stern reaches the outer pilings, and apply forward if needed to stop.

Anytime the boat is in danger of hitting a piling or finger pier, it should be going slowly enough to be easily stopped, so there is no way on if or when you hit. It doesn't matter much how far off the pilings you make the approach, except that hugging too close will swing the stern into one when you put the rudder over. As long as there's enough turning room, you can be as far or as close as you want.

When backing any distance, guard against the tendency to oversteer. Once the stern starts moving one way, it may be difficult to get it going the other, especially if wind is acting on the bow. The steering wheel of ruddered boats should never be spun quickly when you have sternway. Water moving by the rudder from astern can catch it and throw it hard against its stop, turning the wheel forcefully as well. To avoid damage to the steering system (and fingers that may get caught in the wheel), always keep at least one hand firmly on the wheel or tiller when backing.

It doesn't make much difference which lines go on first in a calm, although the usual procedure is to deploy the bow lines, then the stern lines, then springs if necessary. The bow lines may be placed over the pilings from the stern as it clears the outer pilings, then walked forward. Once the bow is centered in the slip, the lines are made fast and the engine(s) may be put slow astern to hold the boat in place until the stern lines are secured (figure 7-2).

Because the width of the stern may nearly match that of the slip, stern lines are often crossed to provide a better lead and more spring (figure 7-3). If the boat is long for the slip, the bow lines may not lead ahead enough to keep the boat from drifting back into the pier. In this case, at least one spring line is called for, from the stern or midship cleat leading forward (figure 7-3).

At some marinas, it is customary to leave your lines on the pilings and retrieve them when you return to the slip. If there's no danger of someone else taking your slip, and you also keep spare lines on board, this may be all right.

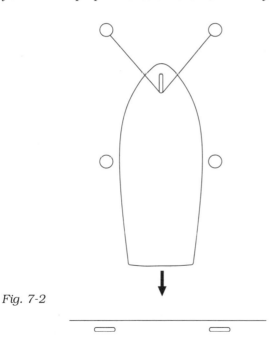

Fig. 7-2

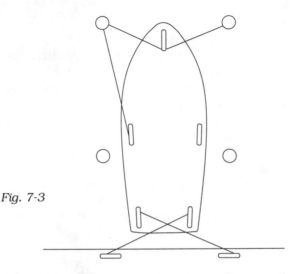

Fig. 7-3

Otherwise, it is necessary to get your lines on the pilings each time you dock. In either case, a boathook should be kept handy for pilings that are out of reach.

If you've made a proper approach, turned, stopped, and backed smartly only to find your stern perfectly aligned with the wrong slip, just pull away and try again. You probably started the turn a bit too soon or too late. It may take a couple of tries to find the right timing in relation to the boat's pivot point.

If there is any wind, it will swing the bow away (downwind) as you slow and then stop. Because the bow presents the greater area to the wind, it gets turned downwind before the stern. For this reason, most boats love to back into the wind, but backing across the wind may require quite a bit of speed to overcome its effect.

Setting Out. Wind blowing out of the slip calls for an approach similar to one you would use in a calm. If the nearby slips are open, you may need a little more speed to cut down on leeway. If the slips along your approach are occupied, the other boats may provide enough of a lee to make this unnecessary.

As you slow and turn away from the pilings, the wind will help swing the bow, so you may not have to turn the wheel much. The wind will make it harder to develop sternway, so use more throttle after shifting to reverse. Once in reverse, the wind will also help stop the boat, so you'll be holding reverse longer than you would in a calm, and shouldn't need much forward power to stop.

As the stern passes between the pilings, bow lines are put on and walked forward. Take up slack until the bow cleats pass the pilings. The lines are eased as the boat continues to back, then held so as to center the bow once the boat is in position. The engine(s) slow astern against the bow lines can keep the boat in place until stern and spring lines are made fast.

Setting Across. With the wind perpendicular to the slip (parallel to your line of approach), it's easy to end up twisted around and sitting against the outer lee piling before you've gotten the boat backed in.

The favored approach is with the bow into the wind, about a boat width off the pilings. Come along slowly, but with enough headway to keep the wind from catching the bow. Shift to neutral to slow down if necessary, and let the bow come a little past your slip before turning away. Once the wind catches the side of the bow closest to the pilings, it will swing you quickly, so turn only enough to accomplish this. Start backing as soon as you begin the turn, and use as much throttle as it takes to gain sternway. The longer you take doing this, the more the wind will turn you.

The idea is to be well into the slip by the time the boat is aligned with it. If you take too long in backing, the wind will blow the bow past the point of alignment and turn you back around the way you came. When this happens, stop the boat and put a line on the outer lee piling, leading it aft to a stern cleat (figure 7-4). With slack out, a couple of turns around the cleat, and a fender in place, back on the line.

It's not necessary to use any rudder with inboard-powered boats since the line and engine are doing the turning. On twin-screw boats, back the engine farthest away from the piling until the boat is straight. Outboards should be pointed in the direction you want to back.

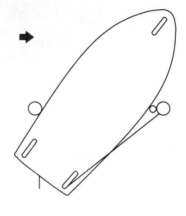

Fig. 7-4

As the line takes a strain, it will warp the boat around until you are parallel with the slip. Start surging the line at this point to let the boat move back. Holding it too long will just waltz you around the piling too far. Get a line on the windward piling to hold the bow up, and once the boat is backed far enough, the warping line may be led forward to the lee bow. Stern lines are applied, and springs if necessary.

Single-screw boats approaching into the wind so that they'll be backing toward their favored side (port for RHP, starboard for LHP), shouldn't go too far past the slip. As you turn, stop, and back, the bow will get blown away from the wind, but the stern will walk toward it and the turn will be quick, before you are set too far downwind.

If you must back to starboard with RHP (or to port with LHP), go a little farther past the slip before turning. As the bow is blown downwind, the stern will walk that way too, though not as quickly. In this case, it will take longer for you to parallel the slip enough to start backing in. Until this happens, you'll be getting set down, so leave enough room to leeward.

In this situation, favor the closer approach of boat A in figure 7-5. Boat B must back across the wind over a greater distance. To do this there must be sufficient speed to keep the bow up, but as soon as you near the pilings and slow down, the bow gets blown to leeward anyhow. To fully grasp this, try backing across a moderate wind clear of any land, docks, or other boats. See how fast you have to go to back straight, and then see how quickly the bow is blown downwind as you stop.

This is a moderately difficult docking situation, so if you don't end up where you want to be, head out and try again. If the wind turns you around before you can get the stern between the pilings, first of all, stop before you hit something. Then get the stern close to a piling (preferably the

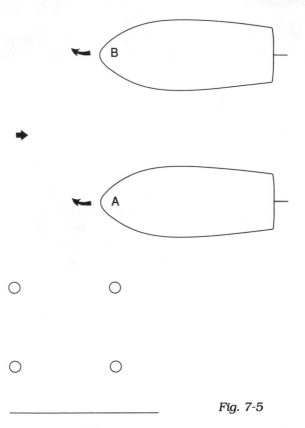

Fig. 7-5

windward one), put a line on, and work the boat in slowly and safely.

A downwind approach is not generally favored since the wind makes it harder both to stop and to turn away from the slip.

The approach is made at low speed, reversing occasionally as needed to slow down. Start turning well before you reach the slip, otherwise the wind will set you past it.

With twin screws, back the outside engine and keep the inside one ahead. Once the turn is complete, back both engines to reach the slip. Single-screw inboard operators should coast in, turn the rudder sharply away from the slip with a short burst of forward to facilitate the turn, then back smartly and use the rudder to steer once sternway is established. Single-screw outboarders should hold forward until the boat is turned parallel to the slip, then start backing toward it.

Favor the windward of the outer pilings, get a line on it, and bring the boat in as you would in the upwind approach. If your bow gets turned downwind and you end up against the leeward piling, put a line on and work your way in as described above.

Setting In. This is the most difficult stern-in situation. As you slow and stop, the wind can catch the bow on either side and turn you around before you are able to reach the slip. It is possible to back downwind into a slip in light to moderate airs, but the maneuver calls for smart boat handling and dexterous line handling.

With the wind blowing straight into the slip, approach along the pilings with just enough headway to turn the bow upwind. Any leeway you make will bring you in closer as you slow, so start the approach more to windward than you would in other situations. You do want to end up fairly close to the pilings when you turn and stop because the shorter the distance you must back, the less time the wind has to act on the bow. Remember to keep enough distance from the pilings to clear the stern when you turn.

For single-screw inboards, approach with the pilings on the side toward which the stern backs. Outboards and twin screws can approach from either side.

Reverse as you turn the bow into the wind. Try to point directly into it as you come to a stop. It can take up to half a minute or so for the wind to catch one side or the other of the bow, but once it does, it will turn you quickly, so use this time to start backing as soon as you can. Employ enough throttle to gain sternway, then throttle down to a safe speed.

If you've aligned yourself properly with the slip, you should be able to hold your wheel steady as you back. If not, steer for a spot between the pilings. It is best to apply a small amount of wheel early than to wait too long and have to turn it hard to correct an extreme situation. Avoid oversteering.

As the stern passes between the pilings, the crew should get a line on each and start walking them to the bow. At this point, you should probably be in neutral. Be ready to use forward gear if necessary to stop, along with rudder to kick the stern to one side or the other to keep the boat aligned with the slip.

When the boat is straight in the slip and the bow lines are on and tended, you can let yourself continue to drift back against them, slacking until you're in place. Adjust the bow lines so that they center the bow under equal strain, then get on stern lines and a forward-leading spring.

When the wind is not blowing directly into the slip, but from either side at an angle up to 45 degrees or so, approach with your bow toward that side. Come a little past the slip and as you stop, turn into the wind—not parallel to the slip. Holding the bow into the wind will give you a few moments to start backing. Once the bow passes through the wind, it will keep going, which is why you don't want to turn so far that you parallel the slip.

As you back in, favor the windward side. Once the stern is between the pilings and a line is on the windward one, you can let the wind catch the bow to straighten you out as you back. If you see that you're going to get set against the lee pilings before the boat is all the way in the slip, take all way off before you hit. With lines on the outer pilings leading aft, you can back in under control until you're close enough to get stern and spring lines on, then lead these lines forward to the bow.

You may have trouble working the stern to windward. If you can get a spring line to a middle piling on the windward side, lead it aft and back on it, easing the windward bow line as you go (figure 7-6).

There are alternatives to backing in under power that you should consider in moderate to heavy wind. The first

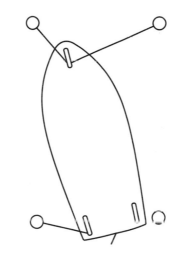

Fig. 7-6

is finding another slip, possibly opposite from yours, so that the wind is blowing out. Two other choices are warping around and using an anchor; these methods are described in chapter 8. Finally, you may consider docking bow in.

BOW IN

Docking bow into a slip is another variation of alongside docking. Since there are pilings on both sides, you can choose the side on which to dock. The approach must be fairly straight because there isn't enough room to come in at an angle and turn the bow away and the stern in as you stop. The more your single-screw inboard backs to one side, the slower you want to enter the slip so as to minimize the need for reverse. With two engines, you'll reverse both.

In a Calm. Bring the boat most of the way into the slip slowly, then reverse to stop. As the widest part of the boat passes the outer pilings, get stern lines on. Once the stern clears the pilings, these lines may be held against a little forward throttle to hold the boat until bow lines are in place.

With a RHP single-screw inboard, turn the bow slightly to port just before reversing, so the boat will stop straight in the slip. You may do the same to starboard for LHP. Twin screws and outboards should come in straight.

As in an alongside situation, if there is any wind, you'd like to have it on the bow for better control. The wind helps to stop you, so little if any reverse is required.

On the Bow. In this situation, the approach should be straight, with just enough speed to keep the bow into the wind. The stronger the wind, the more power you'll need to keep the boat under control, and the more help it will be in stopping. Bow lines should go on first, then stern and spring lines.

On the Stern. With wind on the stern, alongside down-wind techniques apply. Have a line ready forward on each side to place on the outer pilings as soon as possible, usually as the widest part of the boat enters the slip. These lines are then quickly walked aft to secure the stern. Bow and after-leading spring lines follow.

Setting Across. When the wind blows across the slip, favor the windward side, although it may become blanketed by the next boat as you enter. If there's a convenient piling, get an after-leading spring line on and handle the boat as you would alongside. If not, then both bow and stern lines are important.

If you have trouble making the windward pilings or are short of line handlers, just get the boat in as far and as straight as you can and stop as you get set against the lee pilings. From here you can take your time securing.

Bow in has little in common with backing in, where just getting the stern between the pilings is often enough to work the boat in the rest of the way. Docking bow in you pretty much have to get most of the boat in before stopping. Pick one side of the slip to dock, then ignore the other side until you're stopped and ready to get lines to it.

Whether to moor in a slip bow in or stern in may be a question of custom (at some marinas people seem to dock a certain way because everyone else does), convenience (you may prefer bow in for greater privacy or stern in for easier boarding and proximity to shoreside power), ability (people tend to avoid what they find difficult), or conditions (taking into account prevailing, present, or predicted wind).

Most charter companies prefer that you return their boats stern in so that the name on the transom is visible to the cleaning crew and the next charter. If conditions or inexperience make that difficult, no one should complain if you dock bow in, or even alongside at the gas dock, as long as it is done safely.

As skipper, the choice is up to you, and you may take into account several of these factors. The abler you are at handling your boat, the more flexible you can be in different or demanding situations.

GETTING AWAY

Wind direction is the prime consideration in undocking from a slip. Since you are surrounded by pier or pilings on three sides, it's not often possible to just throw off the lines and go. Even in a calm, you may prefer to take lines off and walk the boat out partway before engaging the engine.

Stern In. In a calm, center the boat in the slip, take off the stern and spring lines, and put the engine(s) slow ahead just long enough to gain minimal headway. As the beam passes the outer pilings, bow lines can be more easily retrieved or left behind as the case may be. If the boat is still centered, engage forward gear again and steer straight out, waiting until the stern clears the outer pilings before turning sharply.

With wind on the bow, take off stern and spring lines, then use just enough forward engine to bring the boat ahead. Walk the bow lines aft as you go, but be ready to use them to control the boat. As the beam nears the outer pilings, make sure the boat is centered, take off the bow lines, and use forward power to pull the rest of the way out.

Wind on the stern requires that you first remove the bow lines, then the spring lines, and then the stern lines. Drift out in neutral or with minimal forward power, being careful not to go too fast.

In a crosswind, take off all the lines to leeward and pull on the windward ones to get the boat to that side of the slip. Walk the boat forward a way, holding it to windward as you go. If the wind is light, you may now be able to take off the remaining lines and motor ahead without getting set on the lee pilings. If you see that you are going to hit a piling, take all headway off. Don't try to increase speed and steer your way out if there's any danger of hitting.

In a moderate to strong wind, you must walk the boat partway out. Use the lines to hold it to windward, and when you're sure you'll clear, cast off and apply forward briskly to waste no time in getting away. Remember that steering the bow away from a piling will turn the stern into it. Clear a piling aft by turning the bow toward it, which brings the stern away. Sometimes you have to work your way out slowly, fending off as you go.

Bow In. Operators of twin-screw and single-screw outboard boats should center their boats, then take off all lines and back straight out in a calm. With a single-screw inboard, you may walk the boat partway back, then bring the bow to the side the boat backs. Reversing will straighten the boat out.

When there is wind on the stern, take off bow and spring lines first, then back out as above.

Wind on the bow can be tricky, especially for a single-screw inboard. As you back, the stern pulls to one side, allowing the wind to catch the bow on that side and speed the turn. If this heads you the way you want to go, fine. If not, you may have to accept your fate until the bow is clear, and you have room to come ahead and turn around. In this case, you may either have to back smartly to clear the bow, or take it very slowly and fend off. If you walk the stern lines forward as you back, they can be used to control the bow as it nears the outer pilings.

With twin-screw and single-screw outboards, take off stern and spring lines, then bow lines, and back your engine(s) straight out.

In a crosswind, take off the lines to leeward and pull on the ones to windward to hold the boat to that side. As you back, cast off the bow and walk the windward stern line forward. It can be used to hold the bow to the windward side. As long as the bow is still in the slip, it may be sheltered from the wind long enough for you to back painlessly out. As it exits the slip, the bow will be set toward the outer lee piling. Either use enough power to clear it or have someone standing by forward to fend off.

8. Advanced Techniques

Unusual conditions may require a departure from normal docking procedures that gives you a chance to make creative use of the basic line-handling and boat-handling techniques.

WARPING

Strong wind and current setting off the dock may make it dangerous to attempt docking alongside at A (figure 8-1), especially if you have a single-screw inboard that backs to one side. The answer is to land gently head to the wind against the face at B, then warp around using reverse power, forward-leading spring, and bow lines to end up starboard side to at A. If you have a single outboard, reverse and point it toward A. If operating a twin-screw outboard, do likewise with the outside engine. For a twin-screw inboard, reverse the outside engine.

Warping (using line(s) and engine(s) to turn a boat around a piling) can also work to get you off when the wind pins you against the dock. Come ahead against an after-leading bow spring to swing the stern into the wind (figure 8-2), then back away—or back against a forward-leading stern spring to turn the bow into the wind, then come ahead (figure 8-3). In either case, the line is surged under strain to help the boat around. Make sure that the boat is well fendered.

You may make a decent landing with a strong wind setting on the dock, but wonder if your boat will survive

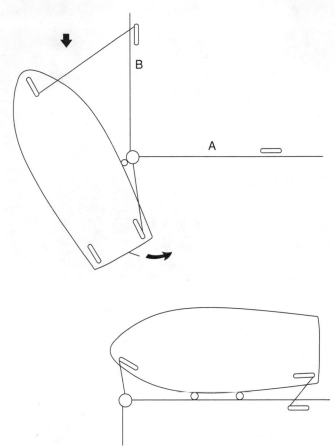

Fig. 8-1

the beating it takes there, and if you'll be able to get away when you want to. A bow anchor can cushion the landing, keep you far enough off to avoid damage, and help you pull off if you need to get underway before conditions change (figure 8-4).

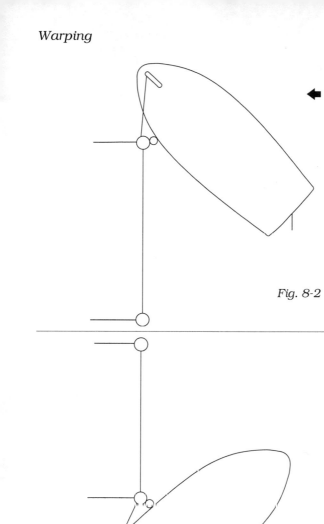

Fig. 8-2

Fig. 8-3

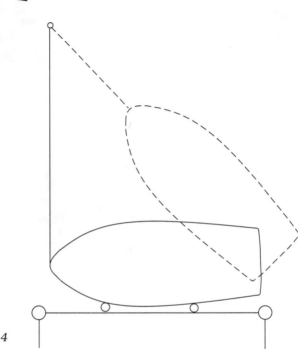

Fig. 8-4

A tough maneuver for any boat is backing into a slip with a moderate to strong wind blowing in. A safe way of accomplishing this is to lay alongside the pilings and warp yourself in.

Approach with the wind abeam, stop at the slip, and let yourself get set against the two outer pilings, broadside to the wind on one side and the slip on the other (figure 8-5). Now you have time to calmly get lines on and work the boat in safely. Run a line from the forward piling aft to the stern cleat on that same side, and a second line from this piling

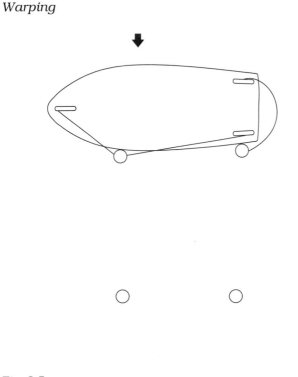

Fig. 8-5 _____

forward to the bow. Lead a line from the aft piling around
the stern to the windward side of the boat (figure 8-5). This
will eventually become a bow line.

Come ahead very slowly, fending off and taking slack
out of the spring line leading forward from the stern. Once
you're far enough ahead for the stern to pass between the
pilings, hold this line and back on it to warp around the
forward piling. A fender should be in place. As soon as the
stern has cleared, start easing the spring enough to let the
boat come back (figure 8-6).

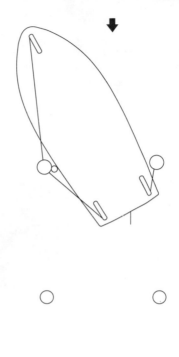

Fig. 8-6 _____

Walk the second bow line forward and let the boat come back against a slight strain on both bow lines as you ease them along with the spring. When the boat is in place, hold these lines and put stern lines on. If the wind is blowing a bit from one side rather than directly into the slip, approach with the bow toward that side, set yourself along the outer pilings, and warp in as above. In this case, the spring line is also used to bring the stern to windward once the boat is well into the slip.

The main advantage to mooring bow out in this type of wind is that you present the bow to the weather, rather than the stern. This softens the strain on your rudder and steering system caused by the waves. You may also prefer that your companionway or cockpit face away from the weather.

BACKING ON AN ANCHOR

What if a boat in one of the adjacent slips sticks out past the outer pilings? You won't be able to lay alongside and warp in. Another method is to bring the bow into the wind, stop about two boat lengths out (depending on water depth), and let go your anchor. As you come back, ease the anchor line, but keep enough strain on it to hold the bow into the wind. In strong wind, you probably won't use reverse at all, and may even need a little forward throttle in the gusts to ease the strain on the anchor rode.

As you enter the slip, put bow lines on and allow them to take the strain. Secure as you normally would. The anchor line can then be slacked off to rest on the bottom, or, if necessary to hold the boat in severe wind, can be adjusted to share the strain with the bow lines. A black anchor ball should be hung forward by day and a white light by night to let others know you are anchored.

Getting underway, you must clear the slip before you retrieve the anchor. Take slack out of the rode as you come ahead, and be ready to hold it again if you need to.

MEDITERRANEAN MOORING

A variation of the above maneuver involves setting a bow anchor and securing the stern to a quay or seawall where

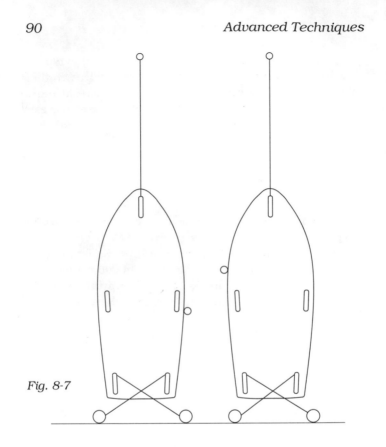

Fig. 8-7

there are no pilings to define a slip. This is often used in Mediterranean and Caribbean harbors where mooring facilities are limited (figure 8-7).

Setting On. In a calm or when wind sets on the quay, stop two to three boat lengths off. The deeper the water, the more anchor line is needed to produce the proper scope (line to depth ratio), so the farther out you'll be. You also want to leave enough maneuvering room to retrieve the anchor.

With the boat perpendicular to the quay and bow into the wind, make sure all headway is off, then drop the anchor. Reverse as necessary to back to the quay, easing the anchor rode but keeping enough tension on it to hold the bow up. When the stern is close enough to the quay, secure the anchor line and apply reverse until the stern lines are secured. A gangway is usually run ashore over the transom.

Setting Off. When the wind blows off the quay, stop as before, perpendicular to it with the bow out. With minimal sternway, let the anchor go and pay out rode as you back. Other than to set the anchor, it isn't necessary to keep a strain on the rode since the bow points nicely downwind on its own. As the stern reaches the quay, hold the anchor line with the boat reversed to keep you in place until the stern lines are secured.

Setting Across. Wind blowing parallel to the quay makes this type of mooring a little more difficult. Setting an anchor and backing on it will point the stern downwind rather than toward the quay.

Approach into the wind as you would if you were going into a slip. As you stop upwind of your berth, turn away from the wind, let go the anchor, and start backing. It helps if the quay is on the side your single-screw inboard backs toward. For a single-screw outboard, it makes no difference. If you're operating a twin screw boat, reverse the outside engine to turn, then use both engines to back to the quay.

Keep slack in the anchor line. The only way you'll be able to steer is with sternway, so the anchor line must not hold you until you reach the quay. An occasional snub as you near the quay will keep the bow from blowing too far off the wind. Once a windward stern line is on, the anchor rode is adjusted to hold the boat perpendicular to the quay.

ANCHOR TURN

Turning against wind or current in a narrow channel can be difficult for any boat, more so for an underpowered single screw. Suppose you're approaching with a strong current behind you and want to turn around to dock port side to at A (figure 8-8). Turning under power alone may not be possible since there isn't enough room to develop sufficient headway to overcome the current. You end up being carried along sideways.

If you have a heavy enough anchor, it can be used temporarily to help make the turn. Approach with the current as slowly as possible. Use reverse if necessary to keep speed over the bottom to a minimum. Start the turn and let go the anchor. Try a fairly short rode to start, but let more out if the anchor seems to drag. As the boat turns broadside to the current, the anchor should start to hold the bow up while the current swings the stern around.

Once the turn is complete, motor slowly ahead into the current to retrieve the anchor, then proceed to dock.

BANK CUSHION

Prop wash from the discharge current of a reversing engine is often used to advantage when maneuvering alongside a solid bulkhead or seawall. Unlike an open slip or wharf, a bulkhead stops water from passing freely, so a cushion of water can be built up between it and the boat.

For example, in docking a twin-screw vessel alongside when the wind blows on, a touch of reverse on the inside engine as you settle against the face sends prop wash

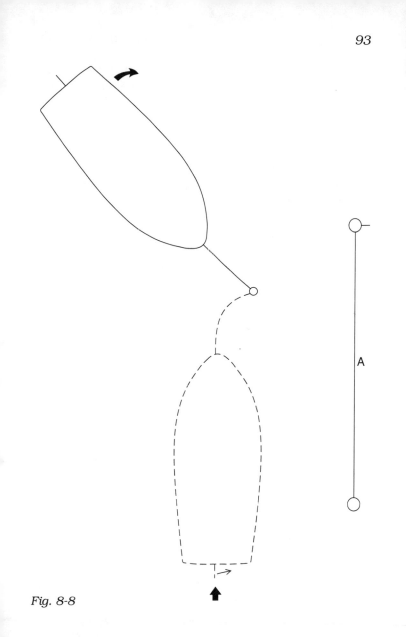

Fig. 8-8

forward between the boat and pier to soften the landing. Reversing the inside engine also pulls the bow in, so keep angled out a bit in the final approach or oppose the inside engine with the outside engine ahead and the rudder away from the pier.

A common technique for getting underway is to first twist the stern out by coming ahead on the outside engine against an after-leading spring, then backing away on both engines. Reversing the inside engine as you come ahead on the outside one will send discharge current forward to push the boat off. Remember to keep the outside engine turning ahead faster than the inside one reverses to hold a strain on the line. Otherwise, you'll move backward before the stern has swung out. Once the stern is clear, reverse both engines, cast off the spring line, and back away.

Single-screw inboards and outboards can, to a lesser degree, also use their prop wash when conditions are favorable.

EMERGENCIES

Two of the problems that can develop during a docking maneuver are loss of steering and loss of power. In many cases, this type of breakdown can be prevented by regular maintenance. In an emergency, it's important to know beforehand that backup and safety equipment are in good order and ready to be used by a knowledgeable crew.

When steering fails, stopping the boat and getting an anchor out may be the soundest action. If there's not enough room for this, you may be able to use the engine to maneuver alongside a piling, get a line on, and then either work your way into a slip or tie up until repairs can be made.

When circumstances permit, twin-screw vessels can be steered with their engines, auxiliary sailboats can be sailed, and all small boats can be maneuvered with an oar—if you have one on board. The nature of the failure, and whether the rudder is stuck in one position or free to move, will dictate your options.

Power failures can happen in different ways. When the throttle cable breaks or becomes disconnected, engine speed can no longer be changed but stays where it was when the cable broke. If this happens at low RPM, then the engine gears can still be changed, so boat speed can be somewhat controlled by shifting between forward, neutral, and reverse. Switching gears at high RPM can cause severe damage. A gearshift failure means that engine speed can still be varied, but the transmission is stuck in forward, neutral, or reverse.

In an emergency, both throttle and gearshift can be controlled at the engine if you have someone on board who knows what to do. Depending on engine location, you may need a third person to relay commands.

As these failures almost always happen in close quarters when control is needed most, there may not be time to do anything but turn the engine off and stand by the anchor rather than continue out of control. This may also be the best response if the problem is in the engine or transmission itself and not in one of the cables.

In almost all cases, there would be more time to react and less chance of damage if you were approaching the dock at slow speed when steering or power failed. The possibility of such failure is a good reason to test steering, engine, and transmission before getting underway, and reverse gear before approaching a dock, especially if you expect to put it to hard use. It's prudent to have the anchor always ready and a trained crew member standing by when

maneuvering in close quarters, since that is when a me-
chanical failure is most likely to occur.

Knowing your boat and crew can better prepare you for
handling emergencies. Each boat has its own idiosyncra-
sies. Pivot points, handling characteristics, and responses
to wind and current vary from one to another. These are
traits that each skipper must first learn, then learn to live
with. Human traits and responses can be shaped to a
degree, but some must also be accepted and lived with.
The ever-present possibility, in fact certainty, of human
error in the docking maneuver makes for infinite variety.
The best preparation is thoughtful planning and the rep-
etition of good habits.

Getting underway is a good time to notice conditions
you're likely to encounter on the way back in. The more
you notice about local wind and current, the more aware
you'll be of how they affect you. Before any maneuver, plan
exactly what you intend to do and how you'll get out of
trouble if the maneuver doesn't work. For example, when
you're coming in fast against a strong wind setting off, do
you have enough room to bail out if your line fails to reach
the dock?

Line handlers play a crucial role in dockmanship. They
should know how to coil a line, throw it, belay it, and make
it fast. They should also be able to act as auxiliary eyes
and ears, advising you of distances and informing you of
things you may not notice. Explaining your plan to them
in advance prepares them and allows everyone to mentally
rehearse the maneuver.

As skipper, it all boils down to your attitude, perception,
and skill. "Any landing you can walk away from is a good
one" may apply to barnstormers, but boaters should hope
for better. Good dockmanship requires study, practice,
instinct, and understanding. Keep your eyes open, and

keep them moving. Early warning means that corrections can be subtle, before drastic ones become necessary. Wind varies, so leave a margin for both change and error. You should ask yourself questions like, "What would I do if I lost reverse now?" Then if you do lose it, you'll know what to do.

Be prepared, but be flexible. Above all, if your approach isn't working or looks bad to you, don't be afraid to turn around and try it again. And again, and again.

Glossary

abaft—behind.

all fast—secure all lines.

cast—turn around in place.

chafing gear—material placed between a line and another surface to protect the line from wear.

check—as you ease a line, hold it momentarily to slow a moving boat.

dip—put the eye of a line through another so that either may be moved without disturbing its neighbor.

discharge current (or prop wash)—water forced out of a rotating propeller.

double—secure both ends of a line on board for quick retrieval.

double up (the bow)—put out a second (bow) line.

ease—pay out line as the boat moves.

headway—forward motion.

hold—have enough turns around the cleat to control a line under tension and keep the boat stopped, but still be ready for further maneuvering.

leeward—away from the wind.

left-handed prop (LHP)—viewed from astern, turns counterclockwise in forward.

let go—cast off, or release.

make fast—secure a line.

pivot point—spot along its centerline on which a boat turns.

point—11¼ degrees, or ⅟₃₂ of a circle

right-handed prop (RHP)—viewed from astern, turns clockwise in forward.

shift rudder—put the rudder to the opposite side.

single up—take off doubled-up lines.

slack—feed line out.

sternway—backward motion.

suction current—water drawn into a rotating propeller.

surge—momentarily ease a held line under strain to let a
stopped boat move.

take up—pull slack out.

warp—use line(s) and power to turn a boat around the
corner of a pier or dock, or around a piling.

way—motion through the water caused by the boat's own
propulsion.

windward—toward the wind, or closer to it.

Index